# CONTENTS MAP

# New Proficiency Writing: an overview

*New Proficiency Writing* provides systematic training in the writing skills required for Paper 2 of the Revised Proficiency examination. The book is divided into six sections covering each of the six different text types: letters, articles, essays, proposals, reports and reviews.

Each unit starts with an exam question so that students can see the task to be achieved. The questions that follow are designed to develop students' awareness of their target reader and their purpose in writing, and the type of format and style which would be appropriate for their text. Students are then helped, through a variety of activities, to build up the sophisticated range of vocabulary and structure required at this level of writing, as well as learning the essential skills of planning and organisation.

At an appropriate point in each unit there is a **model text** which exemplifies the essential features of that particular text type. It is hoped that the teacher and students will see the model primarily as an example of a text type that the student may be unfamiliar with rather than a straightjacket which could be an obstacle to the student's own creativity. The level of writing in model texts has been pitched at a level that students can emulate in their own work, rather than a standard that students might find daunting and discouraging.

# Revised CPE Paper 2: Dos and Don'ts

Encourage students to:
- read the question carefully.
- answer the question in full. If it is a Part 1 question, they must cover all aspects of the question. If it is a Part 2 question, they must give sufficient weight to each aspect of the question.
- brainstorm ideas and make a plan before they start to write.
- organise their text into clear paragraphs or sections.
- connect their paragraphs so that the link between them is clear.
- use linkers to join simple sentences together, but not make sentences too long or too complex.
- use a wide range of vocabulary and structures at the required level for Proficiency.
  (A composition that would get a good grade at FCE would not necessarily meet the required level to pass the CPE exam.)
- check their grammar and spelling while they are writing. They should also allow time to read their writing when they have finished. Examiners penalise basic errors heavily.

Advise students *not* to:
- write out whole compositions or parts of compositions that they have learnt by heart. They are unlikely to answer the question correctly. Examiners will know what they are doing and will penalise them heavily.
- write anything that is irrelevant.
- exceed the word limit. They may make more mistakes and will probably run out of time.
- overuse connectors. This will make their writing sound unnatural and it will be difficult to follow.
- overuse idiomatic expressions, especially where they are inappropriate for the tone or style of text they have been asked to write.

**Pearson Education Limited**
Edinburgh Gate
Harlow
Essex CM20 2JE
England
and Associated Companies throughout the world

www.longman.com

ISBN 978-0-582-52998-4


Set in Wilke and Delta

Printed in Malaysia, VVP

**Acknowledgements**
Designed by Studio Image and Photographic Art
Edited by Tasia Vassilatou
Produced and managed by PROCESS ELT Loukas Ioannou www.geocities.com/process_elt

LONGMAN
EXAM
SKILLS

# NEW
# Proficiency
## Writing

## Teacher's Book

## Mary Stephens

www.longman.com

# Revised CPE Paper 2: Task types

There are six possible task types that students can expect in Paper 2.

## Article

This will be on a theme which would be suitable for publication in a newspaper, magazine, journal or newsletter. The target audience indicated is important as it will influence the register and tone of the article. Some description and narrative may be included. There will usually be a central idea to provide a point or purpose to the writing or reading of the article.

## Essay

Candidates will use the prompt material to produce a composition on a relevant topic. The essay should be complete in itself, with an introduction, body and conclusion and be united by a central idea which provides a point and purpose to the writing or reading of the essay.

## Letter

Formal letters are the most suitable, e.g. a letter to a newspaper giving an opinion and making a point. A letter may include narrative sections to illustrate a point or interest the reader. In Part 2, it could have a narrative focus, e.g. a letter of complaint about an event which did not live up to the writer's expectations.

## Report

The report will have a specified audience, e.g. your boss. It involves the presentation and interpretation, in well-organised prose, of information in relation to a specified context. Candidates may use section headings.

## Proposal

A proposal has a similar format to a report, but whereas a report is an account of something that has happened, the focus of the proposal is on the future, with the main focus being on making recommendations for discussion. Proposals should be well structured with clear sections. Candidates may use section headings.

## Review

A review may be about a book, film, play or place, e.g. a restaurant or hotel. The readership is clearly indicated in the question, and candidates should write in an appropriate register. In addition to providing information about the book, film, etc. the review may embody narrative as well as descriptive and evaluative language and a range of vocabulary relating, for example, to literature or the media.

# Composition marking

## Sample marked text

The following is a sample discursive composition which one student wrote in answer to the question below.

You have been asked to write a composition for your teacher, referring to the extract above (see 'New Proficiency Writing', page 58) and saying whether you think keeping animals in zoos or using for them for research is ever justified and if it is, under what circumstances.

## Suggested correction code

| WW | Wrong word |
| --- | --- |
| WF | Correct word, but change the form |
| SP | Spelling error |
| P | Punctuation error |
| T | Tense error |
| WO | Word order is wrong |
| X | In this line, cross out one word |
| ∧ | Something is missing here |

We like to think that we live in a civilised society yet we are capable still [WO] of great cruelty. A good example

of this can be find [WF] in the way we treat the [X] animals. We keep them gaoled [WW] in conditions which are often

appalling, and we even use them in laboratories in order ∧ test new drugs, cosmetics and other

pharmacetical [SP] products. It is difficult seeing [WF] how this treatment can be justified. As regards zoos, it must

be accepted that a few, usually those in large cities, are worried with [WW] the problem of animal welfare and

do attempt to offer animals the kind of surroundings they are having [T] in the wild. Many other zoos are

not so responsable [SP] and animals in these places are kept often [WO] in tiny cages which offer them little

opportunity to [WW] movement. A lot of animals show signs of distress. But some zoos don't bother about

things like as [X] animal conservation; they exist purely to satisfy the curiosity of the public. It even is [WO] more

difficult to justify the way we treat animals in laboratories. It is very hard for the public gaining [WF] access to

these establishements [SP], which makes people to worry [WF]. There may be a strong argument for using animals

for research into diseases like cancer, but there seems few [WW] excuse for using them to test products like

cosmetics and shampoos. It is unacceptable to keep the [X] wild animals in zoos or to experiment on them,

at least in my opinion. We understand ∧ about animals now than we did in the past. This should make us

to treat [WF] animals with respect. Failure to do so is, I believe, barbaric.

✔ good organisation
✔ interesting vocabulary

Try to use more linking words!
Try to start sentences in a variety of ways!

# Revised CPE Paper 2: Marking criteria

Paper 2 of the Revised CPE examination has two parts. In Part 1 there is one compulsory, contextualised task. Students are required to write one of the following text types in 300–350 words:

- an article
- an essay
- a letter
- a proposal

There is guidance to the context and content from both instructions and one or more short texts and there may be a visual prompt as well. The function of the task in Part 1 is discursive: presenting and developing arguments, expressing and supporting opinions, evaluating ideas, etc.

Both Parts 1 and 2 of Paper 2 carry equal marks. An impression mark is awarded to each piece of writing using the general mark scheme below. The general impression mark is used in conjunction with a task-specific mark scheme, which focuses on criteria specific to each task.

In Part 2, students can choose to answer one of four contextualised writing tasks, including the set book option(s). They will be required to write one of the following text types in 300–350 words:

- an article
- an essay
- a letter
- a proposal
- a report
- a review

There is guidance to the context and content through instructions. The function may be to describe, persuade, narrate, evaluate, make recommendations, give information, summarise, etc.

## Marking: Band scores

Each piece of writing is assigned to a band of between 0 and 5, as described on page 4, and can be awarded one of three performance levels within that band. For example, in Band 4, 4.1 represents a weaker performance within Band 4; 4.2 represents typical performance within Band 4; 4.3 represents strong performance within Band 4. **'Acceptable' performance at CPE level is represented by a band of 3.**

The criteria used by the examiners in awarding marks are:

- realisation of the task set/relevance of the text to the question. (Inclusion of irrelevant material learnt by heart is heavily penalised.)
- range of vocabulary, collocation and expression appropriate to the task.
- stylistic devices: appropriacy of register and format.
- accuracy, appropriacy and range of structure. (Candidates are expected to demonstrate some sophistication of language use. Narrowness of expression and the use of very simple language, although accurate may not be enough to achieve a pass at this level.)
- organisation of text and coherence, including paragraphing and linking.
- development of the topic. (Candidates are awarded marks depending on how ambitious they have been in developing the topic and how well they have achieved this.)
- accuracy of language, including grammar, spelling and punctuation.
  effect on the target reader.

**Note:** Answers much shorter than the 300–350 words required are penalised.
Handwriting that interferes with communication, but does not prevent it, is penalised.
Totally illegible answers receive 0.

# General Mark Scheme
Here is a short guide to the General Mark Scheme.

| Band 5 | Outstanding realisation of the task set: |
|---|---|
| | • Sophisticated use of extensive range of vocabulary, collocation and expression, entirely appropriate to the task set |
| | • Effective use of stylistic devices: register and format wholly appropriate |
| | • Impressive use of a wide range of structures |
| | • Skilfully organised and coherent |
| | • Excellent development of topic |
| | • Virtually error-free |
| | Impresses the reader and has a positive effect. |
| Band 4 | Good realisation of the task set: |
| | • Fluent and natural use of a wide range of vocabulary, collocation and expression, successfully meeting the requirements of the task set |
| | • Good use of stylistic devices: register and format wholly appropriate |
| | • Good use of a wide range of structures |
| | • Well organised and coherent |
| | • Good and ambitious development of topic |
| | • Minor and unobtrusive errors, arising from attempts at complex language |
| | Has a positive effect on the reader. |
| Band 3 | Satisfactory realisation of the task set: |
| | • Reasonably fluent and natural use of a range of vocabulary and expression, adequate to the task set |
| | • Evidence of stylistic devices; register and format generally appropriate |
| | • Adequate range of structures |
| | • Clearly organised and generally coherent |
| | • Adequate, though unambitious, coverage of topic |
| | • Occasional non-impeding errors |
| | Achieves the desired effect on the reader. |
| Band 2 | Inadequate attempt at the task set: |
| | • Limited and/or inaccurate range of vocabulary and expression |
| | • No evidence of stylistic devices; little or no attempt at register and format |
| | • Lack of structural range |
| | • Poorly organised, leading to incoherence |
| | • Little relevance to topic, and/or too short |
| | • Numerous errors, which distract and often impede communication |
| | Has a very negative effect on the reader. |
| Band 1 | Negligible or no attempt at the task set: |
| | • Totally incomprehensible due to serious error |
| | • Totally irrelevant |
| | • Insufficient language to assess (fewer than 20% of the required number of words |
| | • Totally illegible |

# Letters

## 1 Writing to the Editor

### 2 Think about your reader (p.4)

**1** a newspaper article; **2** the editor of the newspaper; **3** the newspaper's readers

### 3 Think about register (p.5)

**b** **complex sentences:** all except: I am afraid I have to disagree.; Furthermore, I would like to remind you … outside towns.; Surely it would be better … towns and cities.

**sophisticated vocabulary used with precision:** raise (a number of) issues, commended, under one roof, accessible, environmental consequences, shopping outlets, inevitably, swallowed up, impact

**passive forms:** out-of-town centres are to be commended; Large areas of the countryside are inevitably swallowed up for development, more roads are built, and pollution is increased

**polite or diplomatic phrasing:** I am afraid I have to disagree.; Furthermore, I would like to remind you

**participle clauses:** Not being a motorist myself, I find these centres anything but convenient.

**relative clauses:** I am writing to you about … shopping centres, which you published last week.; The article raised a number of issues, which I would like to comment on here.

**c** formal

### 4 Identify the key points in the question (p.6)

**a** You are writing a letter (**1**) to comment on the article, (**2**) to respond to the points raised by the article and (**3**) to give your own views on whether we can and should do something about global warming.

**b** **1** The writer suggests that although 'we all worry about' it, we are also resigned to it.
**2** He/She thinks that 'there is very little we can do about it without returning to the "dark ages".'
**3** Power stations, industry, cars, consumer goods that we throw away (e.g. refrigerators, mobile phones, etc.).
**4** We cannot do without these things any more.
**5** 'In the face of all this, is there really anything we can do to tackle the problem?'

### 5 Brainstorm the topic (p.7)

**Suggested answers**

**1** Electricity from power stations makes our lives possible: provides light and heat, powers electrical and electronic appliances and equipment, drives machinery and industry, etc.

Factories supply us with virtually all the goods we need.

**2** They emit waste gases, including carbon dioxide and other poisonous gases. Other liquid and solid waste is dumped into the environment (e.g. rivers, soil, the sea).

If they were not powered by polluting fossil fuels, but by alternative energy sources, they would be cleaner.

Liquid and solid waste could be treated so that it is less harmful to the environment before it is disposed of.

**3** No. Industrially-developed countries consume huge amounts of the world's natural resources. The inhabitants of these countries can throw away goods very easily because they can readily afford to buy new ones.

**4** They poison the atmosphere with their exhaust fumes; roads, parking space, etc. take up a lot of the land area of the planet.

If people made more use of public transport, there would be fewer cars on the road and less pollution; cars could use cleaner technologies (e.g. solar power).

**5** Students' own opinion saying whether it is feasible to put some of the above into effect.

### 6 Make a plan (p.8)

**a** Students should tick all of the notes except:
- habitat destruction
- world poverty

**b** Paragraph 2: Why we should and must tackle the problem

Paragraph 3: How we can reduce emissions from power stations; why we should use fewer consumer goods

Paragraph 4: Other ways to reduce global warming e.g. using cleaner technologies

*Paragraph 5: Conclusion/summary of my views*

### 7 Think about style (p.8)

**1** b; **2** a; **3** b; **4** a; **5** b

### 8 Read a model letter (p.9)

**1** yes; **2** yes; **3** yes; **4** yes; **5** yes; **6** yes; **7** no; **8** yes

### 9 Think about paragraphing (p.10)

**a** *Paragraph 1: Reason for writing: to comment on the article*

Paragraph 2: Why I disagree with the writer – why we must tackle the problem

Paragraph 3: How we can reduce emissions from power stations by cutting down on manufacturing and consuming fewer goods

Paragraph 4: Other ways to reduce global warming

*Paragraph 5: Conclusion/summary of my views*

**b** Yes. Students should underline the following:

Paragraph 1: I am writing to you about the article on global warming which appeared in your newspaper last Saturday.

Paragraph 2: At the start of the article, the writer appears to claim that the situation with regard to global warming is hopeless.

Paragraph 3: In my opinion, we have to work together to persuade industry to cut emissions of gases from factories and power stations.

Paragraph 4: There are other ways we can tackle global warming, too.

Paragraph 5: In conclusion, I want to say that it is dangerous to suggest that all our efforts to tackle global warming are useless.

**c** Yes.

## 10 Think about language (p.10)

**a** Students should underline the following:

(Paragraph 2:) What is more; (Paragraph 3:) However; On the other hand; (Paragraph 4:) too; (Paragraph 5:) moreover

**b** **Contrast:** on the other hand; nevertheless; although; however

**Addition:** furthermore; what's more; moreover; added to this

**c** The concluding paragraph is introduced with 'In conclusion'. Alternative phrases are: All in all, ...; To sum up, ...;

## 11 Think about vocabulary (p.11)

**a** **1** c; **2** a; **3** e; **4** f; **5** d; **6** b

**b** **1** strongly; **2** claim; **3** measures; **4** lead; **5** fail; **6** waste

# Letters

## 2 Supporting an issue

## 2 Think about your reader (p.13)

**1** to the local council

**2** They are responsible for local government and make decisions on local issues like roads.

**3** the inhabitants of the village/region

**4** They can decide that a bypass needs to be built.

**5** in an assertive/firm, but polite way; formal

## 3 Identify the key points in the question (p.13)

**a** **1** in a village; **2** There is too much traffic on it, so it is dangerous.; **3** in a local newspaper; **4** Underline: 'refer to the accident'; 'stating your concern'; 'state your support for the bypass'; 'make a suggestion about what should happen next'.

**b** **1** an accident; **2** outside the gates of the school; the lorry took the bend at the bridge too quickly and skidded and crashed; **3** no (it is the third accident this month); **4** the traffic; to build a bypass; **5** nothing; **6** to support his proposal and write to the council in order to put pressure on them to do something about the problem

**c** formal

## 5 Think about format (p.14)

**1** your address; **2** the date; **3** the name and address of the recipient; **4** the greeting (*Dear X,*); **5** closing phrase (e.g. *I look forwards to hearing from you.*); **6** the ending (e.g. *Yours faithfully,*); **7** your name

## 6 Make a plan (p.15)

Paragraph 4: Say you know that a proposal has been made to build a bypass; why you think this is a good idea; how do other residents of the village feel; suggest what should be done next

## 7 Think about register (p.15)

Mark the following with a cross: aggressive language; a large number of phrasal verbs; idiomatic language or slang; a personal tone; a number of very short sentences; a limited range of vocabulary

## 8 Think about style (p.15)

**1** a; **2** a; **3** b; **4** a; **5** b; **6** a

## 9 Read a model letter (p.16)

**1** yes; **2** yes

## 10 Think about paragraphing (p.17)

**a** Students should underline the following:

Paragraph 2: As you are no doubt aware, the level of traffic through our village has increased at an alarming rate over the past few years.

Paragraph 3: Our village was not built to cope with this volume of traffic.

Paragraph 4: I understand that a proposal has been put forward to build a bypass around the village.

**b** The first paragraph does not follow this pattern. The writer explains, illustrates and develops reasons for writing in the whole of the letter that follows.

## 11 Think about language (p.17)

**1** express my concern; **2** the recent spate of accidents; **3** As you are no doubt aware; **4** day and night; **5** a sharp rise; **6** cope with; **7** pose a (high) risk; **8** take their lives in their hands; **9** a proposal has been put forward; **10** I would strongly urge; **11** take place; **12** put their arguments

## 12 Think about grammar (p.18)

**1** A public meeting is being held at this very moment.

**2** A new proposal has just been put forward and (it) will be discussed by the council after lunch.

**3** Yesterday a teenager who was on his way to school was knocked down and injured (by a vehicle).

**4** Drivers who break the speed limit must be punished more severely in future.

**5** The proposed bypass is long overdue – it should have been built years ago.

**6** Fortunately, a one-way system is going to be introduced in the village next year.

**7** Work on the new road may be completed in a year from now.

**8** When we left the council meeting, the matter was still being discussed by representatives from the traffic department.

**9** We were delayed, so by the time we arrived at the council meeting a vote had already been taken.

**10** The councillor promised that our proposal would be considered again at next month's meeting.

# Letters

## 3 Complaining

### 2 Think about your reader (p.20)

**1** b; **2** c; **3** Tick a, b, d and e; **4** b; **5** a

### 3 Identify the key points in the question (p.21)

**1** You have just returned from another country.
**2** You were on holiday.
**3** You stayed at a hotel in a resort.
**4** A well-known holiday company organised them.
**5** It did not come up to your expectations, you were disappointed.
**6** You have to (**1**) complain about aspects of your holiday, (**2**) outline the reasons for your dissatisfaction, (**3**) suggest what steps you think the company should take to rectify the problems for holiday makers in the future and (**4**) say what kind of compensation you expect.

### 5 Think about register (p.22)

**1** a; **2** b; **3** b; **4** a

### 6 Compare two letters (p.22)

**a** **1** A (does not suggest what steps the writer thinks the company should take to rectify the problems for holiday makers nor say what kind of compensation he/she expects); **2** B; **3** A; **4** B; **5** B; **6** B; **7** B; **8** B; **9** B; **10** A; **11** B

**b** Paragraph 3: Concrete examples of the ways in which the resort did not come up to our expectations

Paragraph 4: Concrete examples of the ways in which the hotel did not come up to our expectations

Paragraph 5: Suggestions about what steps the company should take to rectify the problems for holiday makers in the future

### 7 Think about vocabulary (p.24)

**1** book; **2** over-developed; **3** recommend; **4** assure; **5** picturesque; **6** anticipate; **7** disused; **8** unsightly; **9** indescribable; **10** get hold of

### 8 Think about paragraphing (p.24)

**1** Yes. It clearly states the reason for writing. The writer says that he is writing to complain about a disappointing holiday which he booked with the recipient's travel company.

**2** Students should underline the following:

Paragraph 2: When I booked the holiday, together with two friends of mine, we made it clear to your representative that we wanted a small beach resort which was lively but not too noisy or over-developed.

Paragraph 3: When we arrived at Arosa, we discovered our mistake.

Paragraph 4: Our hotel was equally disappointing.

Paragraph 5: As you can imagine, I am disgusted with the holiday we were sold

**3** The writer says what he expects to be done (i.e. he anticipates receiving an apology and substantial refund from the company). This is important because (**a**) it makes clear what will satisfy him and (**b**) gives the holiday company the chance to rectify the situation, thus resolving matters satisfactorily.

### 9 Think about punctuation (p.25)

(Please point out to students that although the punctuation has been corrected, the letter is still full of errors and flaws.)

Paragraph 2: It cost them a lot of money but they didn't **mind. They** thought we were going to a good place. When we went to the travel **agent's,** the man said that the resort was good for young people but when we got **there,** we found it was full of **boring, grey-haired** old **people. There** was nothing to see and do and nowhere for us to go in the **evenings, so** [optional comma] we were really bored. The hotel was no good because there were no **discos,** just **old-fashioned** singers and entertainers and everything finished by 10.30 in the **evening. We** just had to go to bed and it was really disappointing.

Paragraph 3: The travel agent said that we would have a hotel room with a sea view and a balcony but when we got **there,** our room was at the back and the balcony was so small we could only **stand. We** couldn't sit down or sunbathe. And the view from our room was not of the sea, it was of the back of the hotel where they put all the rubbish. It smelt really **bad,** [optional comma] too.

# Letters

## 4 Writing a personal recommendation

### 2 Think about your reader (p.26)

**1** b; **2** c

### 3 Think about register (p.27)

**a** formal

**b** **adjectives that describe personal qualities:** academically gifted, talented, happy, resilient, popular

**present tenses:** am writing, has been, is, has (consistently) come, is, has (just) been awarded, has shown, is

**relative clauses:** who has been a pupil at this school for the past three years; who is popular with her fellow students and teaching staff alike

**complex sentences:** (the whole extract)

**a range of linking words:** who, and, and, who

**c** formal

## 4 Identify the key points in the question (p.27)

**1** An international aid organisation.

**2** They are an international organisation; they are staffed partly by volunteers; they provide training for volunteers; they do work in less privileged parts of the world.

**3** They would like people to apply to be volunteers.

**4** There are ten requirements.

**5** They will work on projects in less privileged parts of the world.

**6** None.

**7** A young person you know.

**8** He/She wants you to write a letter of recommendation.

**9** Yes.

**10** c

## 5 Brainstorm the topic (p.28)

**1** Students' own ideas.

**2** In your letter of recommendation, you would not really need to refer to the person's age.

**3** Students' own ideas.

## 6 Make a plan (p.28)

**a** Students could group points in a number of ways. One possibility is:

Group 1: adventurous, physically fit, willing to endure harsh living conditions

Group 2: resourceful, practical, able to cope in a crisis

Group 3: able to work as part of a team

## 7 Think about vocabulary (p.29)

**a** inflexible: opposite = flexible

immature: opposite = mature

selfish: opposite = unselfish/considerate/thoughtful/kind, etc.

**b** **1** Jason is *generous* and has done a lot of work for various charities.

**2** He is very *resourceful*, so he can cope with almost any circumstances.

**3** Having worked for a time as a volunteer firefighter, Jason is *tough*.

**4** Jason appears detached but in fact, he is *sensitive*.

**5** He is *self-motivated*, so he can be left to work without supervision.

**6** He is extremely *level-headed*, so he doesn't behave foolishly.

**7** He is *reliable*, so you can be sure he will never let you down.

**8** Jason is *tolerant* and gets on well with everybody.

## 8 Read a model letter (p.29)

**1** yes; **2** yes; **3** yes

**b** Paragraph 1: Reason for writing.

Paragraph 2: My relationship with Jason; why he is suited to what he does at the local youth centre where he is a volunteer (he is committed to helping others, resourceful, able to cope in a crisis).

Paragraph 3: How I know he is able to work in a team.

Paragraph 4: How I know he is physically fit, adventurous, willing to endure harsh living conditions.

Paragraph 5: How I know he is practical.

Paragraph 6: A summary of why I think Jason is a suitable volunteer.

**c** Each paragraph has a topic sentence:

*Paragraph 1: I am writing to you on behalf of Jason Peters, who is applying to work for your organisation.*

Paragraph 2: I have known Jason Peters for four years.

Paragraph 3: One of the most important requirements for us at the youth centre is that we work together as a team.

Paragraph 4: Physically, Jason is very fit.

Paragraph 5: Although he has no professional qualifications, Jason has many practical skills.

Paragraph 6: Jason is a generous, thoughtful and resourceful young man and would seem to fit your requirements perfectly.

# Letters

## 5 Giving an opinion

## 2 Think about your reader (p.32)

**1** to the makers of the television programme;
**2** c; **3** b; **4** fairly serious; **5** formal

## 3 Identify the key points in the question (p.32)

**1** A viewer (i.e. a person who probably watched the programme about young people's habits).

**2** Young people are spending far more time using computers than reading books.

**3** You must:

• suggest why young people are spending far more time using computers than reading books

• give your views on which of the two activities is preferable

• say why this is so

## 4 Think about register (p.33)

**1** b; **2** b; **3** a; **4** b; **5** a

## 6 Organise your notes (p.34)

**b** None of the notes is irrelevant, and therefore all could be included. However, some are not very useful or informative, e.g. 'computers are becoming cheaper to buy'; 'access to a computer is easy'; 'not everyone can afford a computer'.

The student might decide to omit some of the less important points in order to expand on other notes.

## 7 Read a model letter (p.35)

**a** The writer does not include the following notes:
- to play games
- computers are cheaper to buy
- access to a computer is easy
- children can access unsuitable material over the Internet
- not everyone can afford a computer
- multi-media have greater appeal than books
- less time available
- books are cheaper
- it's easier to relax with a book

**b** The writer has covered all points asked for.
She has used the correct format, style and tone.

**c** Paragraph 1: Reason for writing (to respond to the results of the survey on young people's habits).

Paragraph 2: Why young people are using computers more (benefits).

Paragraph 3: Why, in spite of this, computers cannot replace books (comparison between reading off a computer screen and reading from a book).

Paragraph 4: Further problems caused by use of computers (health problems).

Paragraph 5: More problems caused by use of computers (addiction to computer games, anti-social habits, health risks).

Paragraph 6: Both computers and books are valuable.

**d** Students should underline the following:

Paragraph 1: I watched your recent programme and was interested to learn the results of the survey you carried out.

Paragraph 2: The fact that more young people are using computers is hardly surprising.

Paragraph 3: However, there are reasons why computers can never replace books.

Paragraph 4: Another reason for not using computers for sustained periods of reading is for health reasons.

Paragraph 5: A final consideration is the amount of time some people spend playing computer games.

Paragraph 6: I do not for a moment dispute the necessity for young people to use computers but neither must they lose touch with the printed book.

## 8 Think about language (p.36)

**a** 1 e; 2 f; 3 g; 4 b; 5 a; 6 d; 7 c

**b** 1 your findings; 2 decline; 3 a wealth of information; 4 invaluable; 5 indispensable; 6 prolonged/sustained; 7 reflecting; 8 By foregoing

## 9 Think about linking words (p.36)

**a** First of all, …;  A second point to remember is …; Another reason for …;  A final consideration is …

**b** Suggested answers

**1** Although/While computers are now essential to our lives, they will never replace books.

Computers are now essential to our lives. However/Nevertheless, they will never replace books.

Computers are now essential to our lives. They will never replace books, however.

Despite the fact that computers are now essential to our lives, they will never replace books.

In spite of the fact that computers are now essential to our lives, they will never replace books.

**2** Although/While you can look up facts in a book, the process is much quicker on the Internet.

You can look up facts in a book. However/Nevertheless, the process is much quicker on the Internet.

You can look up facts in a book. The process is much quicker on the Internet, however.

Despite the fact that you can look up facts in a book, the process is much quicker on the Internet.

In spite of the fact that you can look up facts in a book, the process is much quicker on the Internet.

**3** Although/While it is true that computers make information easily accessible,  readers can't relax with a computer in the same way as with a book.

It is true that computers make information easily accessible. However/Nevertheless, readers can't relax with a computer in the same way as with a book.

It is true that computers make information easily accessible. Readers can't relax with a computer in the same way as with a book, however.

Despite the fact that computers make information easily accessible, readers can't relax with a computer in the same way as with a book.

In spite of the fact that computers make information easily accessible, readers can't relax with a computer in the same way as with a book.

# Articles

## 6 Describing an experience

### 2 Think about your reader (p.38)

**1** a travel magazine; **2** 'A Great Way to Travel!'; **3** a, c; **4** c

### 3 Identify the key points in the question (p.39)

1 No, it cannot have been boring or disastrous. The two adjectives that tell you this are: 'pleasurable' and 'eventful'.

2 You must give reasons for your chosen means of transport.

### 5 Think about a title (p.39)

**a** **1** e; **2** d; **3** b; **4** a; **5** c

**b** Students' own ideas

### 6 Think about your introduction (p.40)

**Paragraph b** would make a good introduction. It is relevant and to the point, grabs the reader's attention and is well-constructed of more than one sentence, but does not waffle.

**Paragraph a** 'waffles' and has overlong sentences without much 'point' to them. It is not very interesting, either.

**Paragraph c** consists of a single sentence which is not interesting.

### 7 Think about your conclusion (p.40)

**Paragraph a** would make a good conclusion. It gives the reader a sense of closure, carries a punch, is well constructed and longer than one sentence in length.

**Paragraph b** is not a good conclusion. Although it gives a sense of closure, it contributes nothing of interest and is boring and predictable.

**Paragraph c** does not give a sense of closure. It is not well constructed as it talks about the last part of the trip in a rather dismissive fashion and then is rather boring when it talks about having to go back to work.

### 8 Read a model article (p.41)

**a** The text is a good model:

**1** yes; **2** no; **3** no; **4** no; **5** yes; **6** no; **7** yes; **8** no; **9** no; **10** yes

**b** There are many examples of the following features in the article. Here are some:

**an appropriate title:** 'The Journey of a Lifetime'

**addresses the reader directly:** Would you be one of those intrepid types who set off with nothing but a backpack, a map, and a prayer?

**a lively tone:** You bet it did!

**vivid and descriptive:** We rattled through valleys and mountains, peering through grimy windows at the stunning scenery.

**appeals to the reader's imagination:** We visited ruins steeped in history and bustling, modern cities.

**draws on the writer's personal experience:** We learnt to cope with the vagaries of foreign timetables and became adept at communicating by means of hand signals.

**narrative tenses:** In Russia we got lost while we were visiting the Kremlin and were nearly arrested for vagrancy!

**rhetorical questions:** Did the trip measure up to our expectations?

**semi-formal tone:** So take a tip from me when you come to plan your grand tour.

**c** Paragraph 1: How you would choose to travel.

Paragraph 2: Our destination, our means of transport and reasons for choosing it.

Paragraph 3: Description of the pleasurable things we saw and did.

Paragraph 4: The adventures involved in travelling by train.

Paragraph 5: Why the train as a good way to travel.

### 9 Think about vocabulary (p.42)

**1** intrepid; **2** whizz; **3** opt for; **4** agonised long and hard; **5** bucket shop; **6** seductive; **7** measure up to; **8** steeped in history; **9** impervious to; **10** vagaries

### 10 Think about grammar (p.42)

**1** to go; **2** to hop on; **3** setting off; **4** flying; **5** to travel; **6** Backpacking; **7** to settle; **8** travelling;

### 11 Think about tenses (p.43)

**a** In describing aspects of a past experience, you would probably use the following:

Past Simple, Past Continuous, Past Perfect Simple, Past Perfect Continuous, Third Conditional.

The model article uses the following:
Past Simple, Past Continuous, Past Perfect Simple, Present Simple (but not to talk about past experience).

**b** **1** arrived, had spent

**2** stopped, were going

**3** halted/had halted, checked/had checked/was checking

**4** had been waiting, pulled

**5** stole/had stolen, was sleeping

**6** had eaten. had taken

# Articles

## 7 Describing an event

## 2 Think about your reader (p.44)

**1** a quality monthly magazine;  **2** c;  **3** You are asked to (1) describe something, (2) compare it with something and (3) to give your opinion.

## 3 Identify the key points in the question (p.44)

**1** 'Marriage – Past and Present'

**2** A wedding. No, it could not have been boring. The adjective that tells you this is 'memorable'.

**3** You are asked to (1) describe a memorable wedding you have attended, (2) compare it with the sort of wedding your great-grandparents might have had and (3) say whether you think the weddings of today reflect changes that have taken place in the institution of marriage in recent years.

## 4 Think about vocabulary (p.45)

**a** **1** bride, groom;  **2** best man;  **3** bridesmaids;  **4** stag, hen;  **5** registry office;  **6** reception;  **7** honeymoon

**b** **1** got;  **2** conducted;  **3** exchanged;  **4** was held;  **5** made;  **6** proposed

**c** **1** close-knit;  **2** forge;  **3** extended;  **4** single;  **5** vows;  **6** commitment;  **7** sacred;  **8** spouse, stigma

## 7 Thinking about your introduction (p.47)

**Paragraph c** would make a good introduction. It awakens your interest and makes you want to read the rest of the article; it focuses on the theme of the article; it contains a number of sentences that are well linked; it contains sentences that develop one central idea; it will probably lead easily into the next paragraph.

**Paragraph a** is boring and consists of only one sentence that does not develop any idea.

**Paragraph b** consists of a single, rambling, badly constructed sentence.

## 8 Read a model article (p.47)

**a** Students' own ideas

**b** There are several examples of the following features in the article. Here are some:

**1** So much for innovation, you may think.

**2** So how does all this compare with the sort of wedding our great-grandparents might have celebrated?

**3** Just imagine our surprise when the newly-weds stepped into it and were borne away into the sunset, the picture of romantic bliss!

**4** But wait!
So much for innovation, you may think.

**5** Take my cousin's wedding for example.
Later, when *they* had regained terra firma and the reception was in full swing, I got the chance to ride in the hot air balloon.

**6** It took place ...;  The guests, ... sat in rows in front of an altar ...;  the wedding march struck up and the bride glided towards us ...;  The bridegroom, who was waiting at the altar, turned and beamed at her. Soon, the wedding ceremony was under way;  No sooner had the couple taken their vows than the ribbons and garlands were whisked from the altar ...;  when *they* had regained terra firma and the reception was in full swing, I got the chance to ride in the hot air balloon;  It was exciting, ...;  As weddings go, this one was definitely memorable!

**7** altar, elaborately decked, ribbons, garlands, the wedding march struck up, glided, flowered arch, assembled company, beamed, under way, innovation, taken their vows, whisked from the altar, reveal, borne away, romantic bliss, regained terra firma, in full swing, invigorating, conventional, when it comes down to it, in essence, much the same, exchanging vows

## 9 Think about language (p.48)

**1** solemnity;  **2** decked;  **3** struck up;  **4** beamed;  **5** innovation;  **6** bliss;  **7** regained terra firma;  **8** in full swing

## 10 Think about reference words (p.48)

It = my cousin's wedding;  which = an altar;  it = the basket of a hot air balloon;  they = the newly-weds;  it = the ride in the hot air balloon;  this one = wedding;  this = the wedding I attended;  it = my cousin's wedding;  it = the ceremony

## 11 Think about sentence structure (p.48)

**1** The bride arrived smiling shyly.

**2** The bridegroom was standing near the altar waiting for her.

**3** Feeling hot, I went to sit in the shade.

**4** Having finished the service, the vicar left the church.

**5** Waving to the guests, the newly-weds sailed away in their balloon.

**6** Hoping to get something to eat, I went towards the refreshment tent.

## 12 Make your article vivid (p.49)

**1** Can you imagine how amazed we were when we realised what was happening?

**2** Imagine how delighted the newly-weds were when they heard the news.

**3** Picture to yourself how astonished the guests were.

**4** I wonder if you have ever been to a really unconventional wedding.

**5** So what would our grandparents have made of modern weddings, I wonder?

# Articles

## 8 Discussing benefits and drawbacks

### 2 Think about your reader (p.50)

**1** a leading politician's; in a newspaper; **2** a tourist magazine; **3** the readers of the magazine, i.e. the general public; **4** You are writing to give your opinions on the benefits and drawbacks of tourism, and to comment on the politician's statement.

### 3 Identify the key points in the question (p.51)

**1** Yes, on the whole.

**2** b

**3** The holiday maker and the host country have benefited.

**4** The host country has probably benefited economically.

**5** Local communities and wildlife have also been affected by tourism. The adjecctive and phrase are 'unpredictable', 'not always positive'.

**6** 'We must ask ourselves whether tourism on the scale we have it now is a blessing or a curse.'
'On the scale we have it now' = the size and magnitude of the effects of the tourist industry in today's world

**7** A 'blessing' is a good thing. A 'curse' is a bad thing.

### 4 Think about register (p.51)

Put a cross next to the following:
- a formal, scientific style
- a lot of very basic sentence structures
- slang

### 5 Brainstorm the topic (p.52)

**Suggested answers**

**1** It broadens their horizons; it allows them to learn about other countries and cultures and so become more tolerant.

**2** It allows an exchange of ideas and opinions; it provides jobs.

**3** If tourists visit an area to see its wildlife, the local inhabitants are motivated to protect the wild animals and plants.

**4** Development of areas to create tourist resorts and facilities can destroy natural habitats; increased pollution; more people in an area can disturb animals and cause erosion of land.

**5** Tourism can provide jobs for local communities; it can help revive interest in an area; it can encourage investment in an area and improve facilities and services (e.g. hospitals, roads, airports) for the local inhabitants.

**6** The life of an area can be disrupted by over-development (noise, pollution); farming, fishing and other means of earning a living may be incompatible with tourism; an area can become too expensive to live in.

**7** Tourists may initially be attracted to an area because it is unspoilt. However, the tourists themselves contribute to the development (and sometimes over-development) of an area. Soon the reason they came

in the first place no longer exists. There are many such examples all over the world. In the Swiss Alps, for example, tourists come to see the picturesque Swiss mountain villages, However, the Swiss mountain farmers find that they can now earn a living more easily in the tourist industry, and are thus abandoning their picturesque farms. These are falling into decay, and therefore one of the reasons for tourism in the area is being destroyed by tourism itself.

### 8 Make a plan (p.52)

**a** Put a cross next to the following:
- a history of tourism
- how to attract more tourists to our region
- description of my last holiday

**b** **A**
- a section (of one paragraph or more) which deals with the negative or unpredictable aspects of tourism: *2/3*
- one paragraph that leads into the topic: *1*
- a section (of one paragraph or more) which deals with the positive aspects of tourism: *2/3*
- one paragraph that sums up what has been said: *4*

   **B**
- one paragraph that sums up what has been said: *4*
- a section (of one paragraph or more) which deals with the first set of positive and related negative/unpredictable effects: *2*
- one paragraph that leads into the topic: *1*
- a section (of one paragraph or more) which deals with the next set of positive and related negative/unpredictable effects: *3*

### 7 Think about style (p.53)

**Suggested answers**

**1** Many/Some tourists have little respect for the environment.

**2** Many/Some holiday makers can be/are often rowdy and unpleasant.

**3** (Many/Some) developers often build hotels in environmentally sensitive places.

**4** Tourism often brings/can bring wealth to a poor area.

**5** Many/Some people don't care/care little about the environment nowadays.

### 8 Read a model article (p.54)

**a** Outline A

**b** **1** Yes; **2** Yes; **3** No; **4** Yes; **5** No; **6** Yes; **7** Yes; **8** Yes; **9** No; **10** Yes; **11** Yes; **12** Yes

The topic sentences are:

Paragraph 1: The tourist industry is booming, but should we be pleased or worried about its effects?

Paragraph 2: Let's begin with the positive side.

Paragraph 3: If there are so many benefits to tourism, what's the problem?

Paragraph 4: So is tourism a blessing or a curse?

## 9 Think about vocabulary (p.55)

**a** **1** is booming; **2** their natural habitats; **3** rowdy; **4** disrupting; **5** wipe out; **6** subscribe to; **7** impact; **8** lessening

**b** **1** a/e; **2** f; **3** a; **4** a/e; **5** c; **6** d/e

**c** **1** on; **2** in; **3** for; **4** to; **5** on; **6** on; **7** with/by; **8** on

## 10 Think about language (p.55)

**a** Students should underline the following:

It seems …; Let's begin with the positive side; This is of particular importance in …; Another concern is …; Think, for example, of …; The answer must be that it is …; Part of the problem is that …; Perhaps we need to …

**b** Students should underline the following:
Finally, …; To begin with, …

Other items could be:

**Introductory phrases:** First of all, …; Firstly, …; In the first place, …; The first point to consider is …; The first concern must be …; Second, …; Secondly, …; Another concern is …; Lastly, …; The last point to consider is …
**Concluding phrases:** To conclude, …
**Adding information:** in addition, …

## 11 Edit a text (p.56)

Paragraph 1: at; have created

Paragraph 2: people's; prosperity; (may otherwise) have been; whose; by; on; benefited; will (protect); On; worse

# Articles

## 9 Giving an opinion

## 2 Think about your reader (p.58)

1 c; **2** b; **3** b; **4** c

## 3 Identify the key points in the question (p.58)

**1** The subject was the ways in which we exploit animals.

**2** You must consider (**1**) whether you think keeping animals in zoos or using them for research is ever justified and (**2**) if it is, under what circumstances. You must also refer to the extract above

## 4 Think about vocabulary (p.59)

**a** **1** g (d, a); **2** a/d; **3** d/e; **4** f; **5** b; **6** e; **7** c (i); **8** i (c); **9** h

**b** **1** cramped; **2** humane; **3** appalling/barbaric(/cruel); **4** cruel(/barbaric); **5** appalling/barbaric/inexcusable

**c** **1** f; **2** e; **3** d; **4** a; **5** c; **6** b

## 6 Make a plan (p.61)

**a** Students should tick all of the notes except:
- cruelty to pets
- how we use animals to help us, e.g. guide dogs

**b** Paragraph 3: conditions in some zoos; keeping animals in zoos is wrong; how captivity affects animals

## 7 Read a model article (p.61)

**1** yes; yes

**2** Students should underline the following:

Paragraph 1: We like to think that we live in a civilised society, but we are still capable of great cruelty.

Paragraph 2: Take a look at a zoo near you.

Paragraph 3: Now consider the plight of those animals – mice, rabbits, dogs, cats, and monkeys – that are kept in laboratories.

**3** yes; **4** yes; 'Consider the way we treat animals.' 'Take a look at a zoo near you.' **5** yes; **6** yes; **7** yes; examples or explanations follow immediately after all statements; **8** no; **9** no; **10** no

## 8 Think about your conclusion (p.62)

**Paragraph a** would make a good conclusion to the article. It is linked to the paragraphs before it and also links back thematically to the first paragraph. It contains a number of sentences that are well-linked. It summarises the theme of the article and takes it on while at the same time making the article feel complete.

**Paragraph b** links back to only one aspect of the article, which is inappropriate. It consists of only one sentence.

**Paragraph c** links back to only one aspect of the article, which is inappropriate.

## 9 Think about language (p.63)

**1** reputable; **2** pace (up and down); **3** listlessly; **4** breed; **5** endure; **6** plight; **7** admitted; **8** guarantee

## 10 Compare two texts (p.63)

**b** Students should tick the following columns:
**1** Essay; **2** Article; **3** Essay; **4** Article; **5** Article; **6** Essay; **7** Article; **8** Article; **9** Article

## 11 Think about language (p.64)

There are many possible answers for each question. One example is given:

While it might be argued that some experiments on animals are done for medical reasons, the truth is that in the majority of cases they are not.

Although some experiments on animals are done for medical reasons, it must be remembered that in the majority of cases they are not.

Some people claim that some experiments on animals are done for medical reasons. What they forget is that in the majority of cases they are not.

Despite claims that some experiments on animals are done for medical reasons, it is a fact that in the majority of cases they are not.

It may be true that some experiments on animals are done for medical reasons but all too often they are not.

# Essays

## 10 Giving an opinion

### 2 Think about your reader (p.66)

**1** an essay; **2** your course tutor; **3** a; **4** c; **5** to give an opinion; to comment on the extract

### 3 Identify the key points in the question (p.67)

**1** The subject was the causes of delinquency and bad behaviour in young people.

**2** They may be guilty of rowdy behaviour in public, vandalism, drug-taking and theft.

**3** Four possible reasons are: (1) parents are not strict enough with their offspring, (2) the pressures young people face in today's world, (3) the influence of film and television and (4) peer pressure.

**4** Students should underline the following:
(1) 'commenting on the extract' (2) 'examining the reasons why some young people behave badly'
(3) give your opinion as to whether parents should be stricter with children'.

### 6 Think about vocabulary (p.68)

**a** **Adjectives that describe parents:** authoritarian, easy-going, harsh, lenient, strict

**Adjectives that describe young people:** delinquent, disobedient, rebellious, undisciplined, well-behaved

**People:** delinquent, hooligan, rebel, vandal

**Abstract nouns:** discipline, neglect, tolerance

**Verbs:** discipline, rebel, reprimand, scold

**b** **1** easy-going/lenient; **2** discipline; **3** stricter; **4** disobedient/undisciplined(/rebellious); **5** hooligans; **6** delinquents/vandals; **7** rebellious (/disobedient/undisciplined)

### 8 Think about language (p.69)

**a** **1** I firmly believe that … ✓
**2** It's rubbish to say that … ✗
**3** It's stupid to believe that … ✗
**4** It would seem to me that … ✓
**5** You have to be mad to believe … ✗
**6** I tend to think that … ✓
**7** Believe me, … ✗
**8** I am inclined to believe that … ✓

**b** More examples are: In my opinion, …; As I see it, …; I am of the opinion that …;

### 9 Think about style (p.69)

**1 a** over-generalisation  **b** qualifies a statement
**2 a** qualifies a statement  **b** over-generalisation
**3 a** over-generalisation  **b** qualifies a statement
**4 a** qualifies a statement  **b** over-generalisation
**5 a** over-generalisation  **b** qualifies a statement
**6 a** over-generalisation  **b** qualifies a statement

### 10 Read a model essay (p.70)

**1** yes; **2** no; **3** yes; **4** yes; **5** yes; **6** yes; **7** no; **8** yes

### 11 Think about connectors (p.71)

There are examples of the following in the model essay: while, however, although

# Essays

## 11 Presenting both sides of an argument

### 2 Think about your reader (p.72)

**1** a lecture on genetic engineering; **2** from the lecturer's talk; **3** an essay; **4** the editors of your school newspaper, your fellow students, probably members of the teaching staff; **5** to examine the advantages and risks of genetic engineering and give your opinion on whether the advantages outweigh the risks

### 3 Think about register (p.73)

**1** b; **2** a

### 4 Identify the key points in the question (p.73)

**1** Our genes come from our parents. They govern both our physical appearance and our behaviour.

**2** Scientists can now alter genes.

**3** Scientists can make plants more resistant to disease; they can make animals grow larger and healthier; they can treat inherited diseases in humans.

**4** Clones are genetically exact copies of an organism created from the DNA of one of that organism's cells.

Scientists can now clone animals; the first successful cloning of a mammal was Dolly the sheep.

They cannot clone human beings yet, but may well be able to do so in the future.

**5** According to the lecturer, genetic engineering interferes with the natural processes of evolution, and we do not know or understand the long-term effects of this.

### 5 Think about vocabulary (p.73)

**a** **1** f; **2** d; **3** i; **4** h; **5** b; **6** c; **7** g; **8** j; **9** e; **10** a

**b** **Verbs:** alter, avoid, ban, breed, clone, create, crop, design, develop, discover, ensure, govern, harm, inherit, mutate, reassure, research

**Nouns:** alarmist, ban, behaviour, breakthrough, breed, characteristic, clone, consumer, crop, design, evolution, harm, pest, pesticide, research, safety, selection, species, technique, therapy

**Adjectives:** alarmist, amazing, characteristic, genetic, immune, life-threatening, profitable, unacceptable, worrying

**c** inherited; behaviour; engineering; immune; breed; clone; technique; genetically; therapy; design

## 8 Think about connectors (p.76)

Other possibilities are:

**Weighing up and stating arguments:** It think it is true that ...; It is questionable whether ...; I am sure that/I doubt whether ...; It is true that ... On the other hand, ...; While nobody can deny that ..., I would like to point out that ...; I agree that ... However, ...; Although it is true that ..., we must remember that ...; It could be argued that ... However, I would like to point out that ...; Despite all the arguments, I still feel that ...; Notwithstanding the claim that ..., I would argue that ...; It may be true that ..., but ...; Surely it is unacceptable that ...

**Summarising:** In conclusion, ...; All in all, I tend to the view that/I am of the opinion that ...

## 10 Think about your conclusion (p.76)

**Paragraph b** would make the best conclusion. It is linked to the paragraphs before it and also links back thematically to the first paragraph. It contains a number of sentences that are well linked. It summarises the essay and takes it on while making it feel complete.

**Paragraph a** would not make a good conclusion. It consists of a single sentence that adds little of value or interest to the essay.

**Paragraph c** would not make a good conclusion. It does not summarise the essay and in style it is inappropriate. It is clearly an 'add-on' simply in order to say something at the end.

## 11 Think about paragraphing (p.77)

**a** Paragraph 1:  What genetic engineering can achieve now and in the future

Paragraph 2:  The benefits of genetic engineering to agriculture and related risks

Paragraph 3:  The benefits of genetic engineering to medicine and related risks

Paragraph 4:  The future of genetic engineering: designing a 'perfect' human being, and cloning people

Paragraph 5:  Conclusion drawn from points made above – knowledge must be used maturely and responsibly

**b** Students should underline the following:

Paragraph 1:  Over the past decades scientists have made major discoveries in genetic engineering.

Paragraph 2:  One of the greatest benefits in genetic engineering could be in agriculture.

Paragraph 3:  Another advantage lies in the field of medicine.

Paragraph 4:  Some scientists claim that in the future they will be able to design the perfect human being and this might sound like yet another advantage at first.

Paragraph 5:  On balance, it would seem that genetic engineering offers benefits but also tremendous risks.

**c** They = scientists

This = growing crops engineered to be resistant to drought and disease and to natural pests

them = pests such as insects

Another advantage = an advantage of genetic engineering

they = babies with inherited diseases

This = the ability to reduce the risk of developing a fatal disease

this information = the information from a 'gene profile', which would enable someone to see if a person is likely to develop a fatal disease as they grow older

this = the fact that they will be able to design the perfect human being

that = the idea that anyone can judge what is 'normal' and 'acceptable' in human beings and eliminate characteristics they disapprove of

this new science = genetic engineering

# Essays

## 12 Outlining problems and offering a solution

## 2 Think about your reader (p.78)

**1** a magazine article; **2** an essay; **3** You must (**1**) examine some of the causes of stress (**2**) outlining some strategies to cope with the problem and (**3**) say whether you think life today is more stressful than it was in the past. **4** your course tutor; **5** b

## 3 Identify the key points in the question (p.78)

**1** Stress is a disorder which results from living under pressure. It is a problem because it causes various medical disorders.

**2** It may be caused by (**1**) the pace of change, (**2**) doubts about traditional beliefs, or (**3**) living under pressure.

**3** They might be more stressful because (**1**) the pace of change is greater now than it was in the past, (**2**) we have doubts about traditional beliefs, which in the past were the props of human existence and (**3**) we are living under more pressure than our forebears.

**4** Students should underline the following:
(**1**) examining some of the causes of stress,
(**2**) outlining some strategies to cope with the problem, (**3**) respond to the questions posed in the article, (**4**) say whether you think life today is more stressful than it was in the past

## 4  Think about your vocabulary (p.79)

**a**  **1** strategies;  **2** niggling;  **3** frenetic;  **4** relief;
**5** evolved;  **6** allay;  **7** uproot;  **8** ties

**b**  **1** d;  **2** e;  **3** b;  **4** f;  **5** c;  **6** a

**c**  **1** trembling fingers;  **2** emotional support;
**3** sweaty palms;  **4** irrational fears;  **5** deep breathing;
**6** chronic stress

## 7  Read a model essay (p.81)

**b**  **Paragraph a** would make the better conclusion. It is
linked to the paragraphs before it, and also links back
thematically to the first paragraph. It contains two
well linked sentences and makes the essay feel
complete.

**Paragraph b** consists of only one sentence and is a
rather lame way of finishing an essay.

**c**  **1** Yes;  **2** No;  **3** Yes;  **4** No;  **5** No;  **6** Yes;  **7** No;
**8** Yes;  **9** No;  **10** No

**d**  Paragraph 1:  The symptoms of stress; what is stress?

Paragraph 2:  The survival value of stress for animals
and primitive people – facing physical
danger.

Paragraph 3:  The causes of stress in the modern
world are mental rather than physical:
the results.

Paragraph 4:  Strategies to combat stress.

Paragraph 5:  Summary and conclusion.

**e**  Yes, the writer has included topic sentences.
Students should underline the following:

Paragraph 1:  Most of us feel stressed at some time in
our lives.

Paragraph 2:  Stress is nothing new.

Paragraph 3:  The world has changed, however, and
the sort of stress we experience
nowadays is mental rather than
physical.

Paragraph 4:  Fortunately, there are strategies we can
adopt to mitigate or even dispel the
effects of stress.

Paragraph 5:  The world today is changing and
developing at such a rapid pace that it
is bound to leave us feeling stressed
and anxious.

## 8  Think about grammar (p.82)

**1**  We live in a world which/that often seems
unpredictable and uncontrollable.

**2**  People who/that have been forced to uproot
themselves to search for work lack emotional support
in times of crisis.

**3**  Stress is a reaction to a threat which/that can be real
or perceived.

**4**  There are recognisable symptoms of stress, which we
have all experienced.

**5**  Some people who/that fail to cope with stress can
become seriously ill.

**6**  Stress relievers are activities which/that relieve the
effects of stress.

## 9  Think about language (p.83)

Students should underline the following:

Anyone who has ... will (recognise) ...;  Fortunately,
there are (strategies we can adopt)

# Proposals

## 13  Writing a proposal (1)

## 2  Think about your reader (p.84)

**1** c;  **2** a;  **3** to make suggestions, to recommend
something, to put forward ideas

## 3  Think about register (p.85)

**a**  Students  should tick the following:
- impersonal statements
- passive forms
- complex sentences
- a tentative, diplomatic style
- a sophisticated vocabulary, used with precision

**b**  **1** a;  **2** b;  **3** b;  **4** a;  **5** a;  **6** a

## 4  Identify the key points in the question (p.85)

**1**  a tourist office

**2**  Tourists (**a**) from your own country and (**b**) from
abroad

**3**  It will benefit the local economy.

**4**  He/She wants you to outline some ways of improving
amenities.

**5**  • How to attract tourists (**a**) from our own country
and (**b**) from abroad.
- Write a proposal on ways to attract more tourists.
- Outline some ideas on how to improve tourist
amenities in the area.

## 7  Think about your introduction (p.86)

**Paragraph b** would make the best introduction. It is in
an appropriate register, it is brief and clear and makes the
topic of the proposal immediately clear to the reader. (It
is good office and business practice not to waste the
reader's time by forcing them to read through the text
looking for the topic of a proposal.)

**Paragraph a** would not make a good introduction. It
does not make clear what the proposal is about. It is in
not in an appropriate register, either.

**Paragraph c** would not make a good introduction,
either. It is in an inappropriate register.

## 8 Think about your conclusion (p.87)

**Paragraph a** would make the better conclusion. It is in an appropriate register and is brief and clear. It rounds off the proposal by justifying the recommendations made and entrusts the conclusions to the reader.

**Paragraph b** would not make a good conclusion. It is not in an appropriate register. Neither does it justify the recommendations made.

## 9 Compare two proposals (p.87)

**1** A and B; **2** B; **3** B; **4** B; **5** B; **6** B; **7** B; **8** B; **9** B; **10** B

## 10 Think about language (p.89)

Students should underline the following:

I propose we (should) …;  We could …;  One (solution) might/would be to …;  Another possibility would be to …;  I would like to see …

# Proposals
## 14 Writing a proposal (2)

## 2 Think about your reader (p.90)

**1** the directors of the charity;  **2** to make recommendations; to give your opinion, to hypothesise about the results of the action you recommend;  **3** a

## 3 Identify the key points in the question (p.91)

**1** an international charity

**2** an anonymous donation of £200,000

**3** the directors

**4** • to target this sum on one large project *or* on several smaller ones

• to use the money now *or* to keep some of the funds in reserve to be used in future emergencies

**5** You must:
• suggest how the funds should be allocated
• say which projects should benefit
• give your justification for the expenditure

## 4 Think about vocabulary (p.91)

**b** (Suggested answer) *Hurricanes*, *floods*, earthquakes, droughts, famine, epidemics, storms (e.g. tornadoes, hurricanes, cyclones, blizzards), fires

**c** **1** donation; **2** raise; **3** appeal; **4** malnourished; **5** distressing; **6** urgent; **7** desperate; **8** victims

**d** **1** e; **2** a; **3** f; **4** b; **5** d; **6** c/f

**e** **1** urgent action; **2** desperate plight; **3** humanitarian crisis; **4** worthwhile cause; **5** starving/desperate people; **6** disaster zone

## 6 Make a plan (p.93)

**a** **1** ✓; **2** ✓; **3** ✗; **4** ✓; **5** ✗

**b** This helps the writer to focus on what he or she has to say and to write clear paragraphs. This helps the reader by making the proposal easy and clear to follow.

## 7 Read a model proposal (p.94)

**1** yes

**2** yes

**3** The proposal is on the topic asked for. The writer has not written anything irrelevant.

**4** She has used a range of complex structures correctly.

**5** There is a good range of vocabulary.

**6** yes

**7** yes

**8** yes

## 8 Think about your conclusion (p.95)

**Paragraph b** would make a good conclusion. It is in an appropriate register and is brief and clear. It rounds off the proposal by justifying the recommendations made and entrusts the conclusions to the reader.

**Paragraph a** would not make a conclusion. It is not in an appropriate register. Neither does it justify the recommendations made.

## 9 Think about language (p.95)

**1** Examples of hypothetical statements are:

… it would be impossible as well as undesirable …

The extra funds would allow us to buy medicines …

With the funds available, we could improve conditions in these camps …

These volunteers would work alongside drug users …

It would also be possible to set up more centres …

**2** Students should underline the following:

I believe …;
I feel strongly that

**Possible alternatives:**

Personally I feel that … Let me explain why.

In my opinion, …

As I see it, …

It seems to me that …

I would argue that … for the following reasons.

I am convinced that …

I am of the opinion that …

I am very much in favour of/against …

I am completely opposed to …

The reasons why I believe that … are as follows.

**3** Yes. Examples are:

However, given that such a fund already exists, and that we can expect to raise more money in emergency appeals as and when the occasion arises, I suggest that we put this unexpected gift to immediate use.

I believe it would be impossible as well as undesirable to favour one single project, or, indeed one country, above others. For that reason, I would recommend …

Africa must continue to be one of our top priorities. Millions of people are threatened by Aids, … The extra funds would allow us to buy medicines, …

War and drought have forced people … into refugee camps. With the funds available, we could improve conditions in these camps …

Drugs are ruining the lives of young people …, so I feel strongly that we should allocate some of the funds to train volunteers.

**b** **1** allocate; **2** reserve funds; **3** In the event of; **4** as and when the occasion arises; **5** to favour … above …; **6** one of our top priorities; **7** conquer their addiction; **8** give it due consideration

## 10 Think about grammar (p.96)

**b** **1** allocating; **2** that we approach; **3** to raise; **4** to be; **5** funding; **6** that we use; **7** to invest; **8** to use

**c** **1** that one of our representatives (should) go out/goes out

**2** that well-known public figures (should) make/makes

**3** that people (should) make

**4** that the public (should) help/helps

**5** spending

# Proposals
# 15 Writing a proposal (3)

## 2 Think about your reader (p.98)

**1** a large company;  a staff representative;

**2** a memo; one of the managers; **3** c; **4** a; **5** to explain the reason for a state of affairs, to suggest ways to deal with the problems, and to justify any expenditure involved

## 3 Identify the key points in the question (p.99)

**a** You must (1) suggest ways to deal with the problems outlined in the extract and (2) justify any expenditure involved.

**b** **1** Members of staff tend to lead unhealthy lifestyles. Many people exist on a diet of fast foods. Few exercise as they should, with the majority spending their free time in sedentary activities. The writer implies that the food they eat is not healthy and that they do not exercise enough.

**2** The result is that people are unfit and unhealthy. Obesity may be a problem and there is an increased incidence of heart disease.

**3** The writer thinks the company should take urgent steps to encourage its workforce to become fitter and healthier.

## 4 Think about format (p.99)

Students should tick the following;

- text divided into sections
- headings
- sub-headings
- an impersonal tone
- recommendations for future actions
- complex sentences
- hypothetical statements
- sophisticated vocabulary used with precision
- passive forms

## 5 Think about vocabulary (p.99)

**a** The verb that collocates with all the phrases is 'take'.

**b** Possible answers are:

**1** begin/start, have, launch, organise

**2** begin/start, have, hold, organise

**3** advise, encourage, help, make, tell

**4** build, construct, have, plan

**5** justify, make up for, offset

**c** **1** campaign; **2** practical; **3** common; **4** benefits; **5** facilities; **6** substantial

## 8 Compare two proposals (p.101)

Both proposals cover the points asked for in the exam question. However Proposal A is better for the following main reasons:

(1) It is written in the correct format for a proposal, with clear headings and subheadings.
Proposal B is in an incorrect format, partly proposal format and partly letter format.

(2) Proposal A uses an appropriate style and register throughout, whereas Proposal B does not. Examples of inappropriate language are: 'do not have a clue', 'I reckon', 'Why not get staff to …'.

(3) Proposal A uses a good range of vocabulary correctly and a number of complex sentences. Proposal B, on the other hand, is written using largely basic vocabulary and simple sentences.

(4) Proposal A has an appropriate introduction and conclusion, whereas Proposal B does not.

Proposal A has the right number of words, whereas Proposal B is too short.

## 9 Think about language (p.102)

**a** Words and phrases to make recommendations:
I recommend that …; we should …; I propose
that …; I suggest

Words and phrases to make hypothetical
statements: If we were to …, would; (Staff) would
(have)

**b** **1** submitting; **2** staff/workforce; **3** In the meantime;
**4** are in the habit of working; **5** It is common
practice; **6** commute considerable distances; **7** offset

# Reports

## 16 Writing a report (1)

## 2 Think about your reader (p.104)

**1** c; **2** a; **3** to describe something, to make suggestions;
**4** You must (**1**) review the complaints and (**2**) suggest
how the situation can be improved.

## 3 Think about format (p.104)

Template B is suitable for a report.

## 4 Brainstorm the topic (p.105)

**a** Suggested answers

The lift is out of order.

There is no porter to carry the guests' luggage.

The receptionists ignore the guests.

There are workmen making a lot of noise.

There is litter on the floor.

The hotel is old and in a state of disrepair.

The staff chat together instead of serving the guests.

## 5 Think about vocabulary (p.106)

**a** **1** g; **2** j; **3** h; **4** i; **5** b; **6** a; **7** c; **8** e; **9** f; **10** d

**b** **1** noisy; **2** stuffy; **3** filthy; **4** out of order;
**5** cramped; **6** rude; **7** exorbitant; **8** inedible

**c** **1** b; **2** a; **3** e; **4** d; **5** f; **6** c

**d** **1** fix/repair; **2** dismiss/fire; **3** installing/putting in;
**4** looked into/investigated; **5** propose/recommend;
**6** disregard/ignore

## 6 Think about style (p.107)

**b** **1** b; **2** b; **3** b; **4** a; **5** b; **6** a; **7** a; **8** a

**c** **1** Some guests have been disregarding the no
smoking sign.

**2** Guests were allocated special rooms on the ground
floor.

**3** I propose (that) we (should) ban smoking in the
restaurant. / I propose (that) smoking (should) be
banned in the restaurant.

**4** Most of the problems have been rectified. / We have
rectified most of the problems.

**5** We have experienced difficulty (in) getting staff.

**6** The staff are unable to cope.

## 8 Read a model report (p.109)

The model is well written. It has all the features in the
checklist.

## 9 Link your text (p.110)

**a** they = the radiators

This = the disco

it = the disco

they = non-residents

it = the disco

the problem = noise from the disco

here = in the restaurant

in this area = the long delays in getting served at
peak times

This = smoking

this area = the no smoking zone

**b** **1** While, nevertheless; **2** consequently; **3** Although;
**4** Overall; **5** Nevertheless; **6** whereas

## 10 Think about vocabulary (p.110)

**1** In the interim; **2** restrict; **3** peak times; **4** our full
complement of staff; **5** envisage; **6** persist;
**7** implement; **8** designate; **9** rectified; **10** outstanding
issues

# Reports

## 17 Writing a report (2)

## 2 Think about your reader (p.112)

**1** c; **2** to give information about the two restaurants;
**3** in order to be able to recommend them to visitors both
from your own country and abroad; **4** b

## 3 Identify the key points in
the question (p.112)

**1** two; **2** contrasting ones; **3** good ones; **4** both
restaurants; **5** You must include (a) comments on the
size and location of the restaurants and (b) comments on
the atmosphere, service and type of dishes served.

## 4 Think about vocabulary (p.113)

**a** **Positive or neutral adjectives**: crisp, delicious,
exotic, fresh, healthy, imaginative, melt-in-the-mouth,
mouth-watering, plain*, raw*, spicy, stunning,
succulent, superb, tender

**Negative adjectives**: disappointing, dried-up, fatty,
greasy, limp, over-cooked, stale, tasteless, tough

*'plain' and 'raw' could be used with a negative
meaning depending on the context.

**b** delicious/tasteless, tender/tough, exotic/plain, fresh/stale, spicy/plain

**c** **Size**: cramped, roomy, spacious

**Price**: pricey, reasonably-priced, over-priced

**Service/Staff**: attentive, courteous, efficient, friendly, offhand

**Location**: central. convenient, off the beaten track

**Atmosphere**: cosy, friendly, sophisticated

**d** **1** pricey; **2** sophisticated; **3** tender/succulent; **4** courteous; **5** mouth-watering/delicious/superb; **6** off the beaten track; **7** spicy; **8** cosy

## 5 Brainstorm the topic (p.114)

**a** **Suggested answers**

Encourage students to use their imagination when answering these questions.

**The Lemon Tree**: elegant, formal, spacious, courteous service, pricey

**The Green Lodge**: relaxed, cosy, homely, off the beaten track, reasonably priced, delicious home-made fare

**b** **The Lemon Tree**

**Size**: spacious, seats about 100 diners

**Location**: in the centre of town

**Type of dishes**: extensive menu, succulent steaks, superb fish dishes

**Prices**: pricey – around £40 per person

**Staff and service**: formal and attentive

**Atmosphere**: romantic, candlelit atmosphere, glass chandeliers and a huge log fire. Music provided most evenings by a first-class string ensemble.

**The Green Lodge**

**Size**: small but not cramped, seats about 40 max

**Location**: off the beaten track

**Type of dishes**: home-cooked, traditional local recipes, mouth-watering desserts

**Prices**: very reasonable

**Staff and service**: genuine hospitality offered by owner Manuel and his wife

**Atmosphere**: cosy, intimate atmosphere where diners can relax. There are real log fires and on most evenings live entertainment usually in the form of a classical guitarist.

## 7 Think about style (p.115)

Students should underline the following:
great big; really, really popular; posh; popped in; like a dog's dinner; the fright of my life; really pricey; great; I suppose

## 8 Make a plan (p.116)

**b Suggested answers**

Encourage students to use their imaginations to develop their own plans.

**Introduction:**

Have visited both restaurants and prepared the following report.

**Size and location:**

Restaurant X = small, seats about 40 max. Tucked away in back streets of the town, near the artists' quarter.

Restaurant Y = vast, on two floors, seats about 100. Situated on one of the main avenues leading into the town. A popular tourist area.

**Types of dishes and prices:**

Restaurant X = delicious home-made fare, using guaranteed organic produce. Local dishes cooked according to traditional recipes. Mouth-watering desserts. Great value for money.

Restaurant Y = Elegant dishes. Wide variety. Fish a speciality. Pricey but worth it for that special occasion.

**Service:**

Restaurant X = Family-run restaurant. service friendly and attentive.

Restaurant Y = Formal but very efficient.

**Atmosphere:**

Restaurant X = cosy, homely feel. Very intimate.

Restaurant Y = elegant, beautifully decorated but rather cold.

**Conclusion:**

Restaurants quite different but both excellent in their own ways. No hesitation in recommending them both.

## 9 Think about your introduction (p.116)

**a** **To:** Tourist Office Manager
**From:** your name
**Date:** today's date
**Subject:** Recommendations for restaurants in the town

**b** The appropriate introduction is Number 3. Number 1 is too informal. Number 2 is too short. Number 4 is unclear and too long.

**c** **Suggested answers**

**1** I have now visited both of the leisure centres we were considering for our staff scheme and have prepared the following report and recommendations for your consideration.

**2** This report contains information about both of the schools we were considering for our students and my recommendations.

## 10 Think about your conclusion (p.117)

The appropriate conclusion is 3. Conclusion 1 is inappropriate because the question asks for a report on two restaurants that you would *recommend*. Conclusion 2 is too casual. Conclusion 4 is rather confusing.

## 11 Edit your text (p.118)

**Introduction:** on; recommend; in

**Size and location:** spacious, airy; in; seat; inside and on the terrace at the back, …; view; small, family restaurant; on; worth visiting; a marvellously relaxed and cosy atmosphere; seat; although; in; permits

**Types of dishes:** caters; caviar, wild salmon; variety; desserts; Although; does offer/offers; menu

**Atmosphere and service:** both elegant and sophisticated

**Prices:** much higher; give good value

**Conclusion:** both to be excellent; in

# Reviews

## 18 Writing a film review

### 2 Think about your reader (p.120)

**1** b; **2** nothing, except they are interested in the media; **3** c; **4** b; **5** to compare two things, to give an opinion; to justify your views; to inform; to interest

### 3 Identify the key points in the question (p.120)

You must (**1**) write a review of a film that is based on a novel (**2**) and comment on how successful the dramatisation has been.

### 4 Think about vocabulary (p.121)

**a 1** shot; **2** cast; **3** directed; **4** theme; **5** based; **6** villain; **7** scene; **8** set

**c 1** scene; **2** character; **3** atmosphere; **4** cuts; **5** turn; **6** spell-binding; **7** unfolds; **8** climax; **9** foreboding; **10** escape

### 6 Make a plan (p.122)

Paragraph 4: How successful was the dramatisation.

### 7 Read a model review (p.123)

**a** The model is well written. It has all the features in the checklist.

**b** Yes, both parts of the exam question are covered. The writer gives enough attention to both areas. Paragraphs 2 and 3 review the film itself. Paragraph 4 comments on the issue of how successful the dramatisation has been.

**c** The writer uses present tenses.

**Present Simple:** they apologise frequently; Captain Corelli, hates war; He is billeted; the two young people are attracted to each other; events take an unexpected turn

**Present Continuous:** The Italian army are occupying Cephalonia; Although they are clearly enjoying the local delights

**d** The writer uses the Present Simple and Present Perfect: The book is long and is rich; Only a few of these are portrayed; the cuts have been quite drastic; Nicholas Cage does not fit the description of Corelli; The problem … is that readers have built a picture

**e** Yes, there is. The topic sentences are:

Paragraph 1: *Captain Corelli's Mandolin* is the latest blockbuster to hit our cinemas.

Paragraph 2: It is, at heart, a love story.

Paragraph 3: Directed by John Madden, the film captures all the beauty of the Greek island, with its clear blue skies and sun-drenched beaches.

Paragraph 4: While film-goers will undoubtedly love the film, those who have read the novel may feel disappointed.

### 8 Think about vocabulary (p.124)

**1** idyllic; **2** at ease; **3** genial; **4** drastic; **5** squaring

### 9 Think about language (p.124)

**a 1** While film goers will love the film, readers of the novel may feel disappointed.

**2** Despite being already engaged, the heroine falls in love with an Italian soldier. / Despite the fact that the heroine is already engaged, she falls in love with an Italian soldier.

**3** Although Captain Corelli is a soldier, he hates war.

**4** In spite of the fact that the film covers fewer events, it is just as exciting as the book. / In spite of the film covering fewer events, it is just as exciting as the book.

**5** Whereas the novel highlights the role played by other countries in the war, the film glosses over those details.

# Reviews

## 19 Writing a book review

### 2 Think about your reader (p.126)

**1** a; **2** a; **3** to interest; to inform; to evaluate

### 3 Identify the key points in the question (p.126)

**1** a book; **2** for children; **3** you are impressed; **4** the features that make it an ideal book for children; **5** Students should underline the following:
(1) Write a review of the book for a magazine and
(2) comment on the features that make it an ideal book for children.

### 4 Think about vocabulary (p.127)

**a 1** title; **2** marvellous; **3** illustrated; **4** cast; **5** plot; **6** scene; **7** chapters, cliff-hanger; **8** hardback, paperback

**b 1** humorous; **2** gripping; **3** convincing; **4** intriguing; **5** inventive

**c 1** I was not able to stop reading because it gripped my attention.

**2** a development in the story that took me by surprise because I was not expecting it

**3** makes you believe something that turns out to be wrong or different from what you expected

**4** I must not tell you so much that you are able to guess what happens.

**5** was as good as I expected it to be

## 6 Make a plan (p.128)

**Suggested answers**

Paragraph 2: Outline of the plot

Paragraph 3: Comment on the main characters and why they are appealing

Paragraph 4: The features that make the book ideal for children

## 7 Compare two reviews (p.129)

**1** A and B (however, the register in B is inappropriate); **2** A; **3** A; **4** A; **5** A and B; **6** A; **7** A; **8** A; **9** A and B; **10** A and B

## 8 Think about language (p.130)

**1** archetypal; **2** picks; **3** permeates; **4** large; **5** prey; **6** forces; **7** cliff-hanger; **8** drawn; **9** sensitive/vulnerable; **10** swot; **11** thick; **12** ingenuity

## 9 Think about tenses (p.131)

**Present Simple:** is; suck out; are forced; ends; keeps
**Present Continuous:** is being hunted
**Present Perfect:** has escaped

# Reviews

## 20 Writing a review of a place

## 2 Think about your reader (p.132)

**1** to criticise some aspects of a hotel, to praise other aspects of it, to describe and evaluate it; **2** b

## 3 Identify the key points in the question (p.132)

**1** a new hotel; **2** you were shown around it; recently; **3** Some aspects impressed you but you also found aspects to criticise.

## 4 Think about vocabulary (p.133)

**a** **1** chilly/warm; **2** cramped/spacious; **3** disappointing/superb; **4** filthy/immaculate; **5** huge/tiny; **6** impersonal/intimate; **7** luxurious/spartan; **8** off-putting/welcoming

**b** **1** immaculate; **2** luxurious/superb; **3** cramped; **4** intimate/warm/welcoming; **5** off-putting/chilly; **6** chilly/impersonal/spartan

## 6 Make a plan (p.134)

Paragraph 3: Areas that need improving

## 7 Read a model review (p.134)

**a** The answer to all questions is 'yes'. For question 5, the topic sentences are as follows:

Paragraph 1: Those who are searching for a good hotel need look no further than *The Star.*

Paragraph 2: When I toured the hotel, I was impressed by the spaciousness of the accommodation.

Paragraph 3: While *The Star* has much to recommend it, some areas could be improved.

Paragraph 4: In spite of these few criticisms, my overall impressions of the hotel were extremely favourable.

**b** yes

## 8 Think about language (p.135)

All the phrases in the box have been used, except 'I was disappointed to find that …'.

## 9 Think about grammar (p.136)

**1** Located in the centre of the town, the hotel is very convenient for the shops.
**2** Designed by a famous architect, the building dominates the centre.
**3** Overlooking the sea, the restaurant is a superb place to eat.
**4** Built to Olympic standards, the swimming pool is a star feature of this hotel.

# Set books

In Paper 2, Part 2, students may choose to answer one question from a selection of the set books. Students should not attempt to answer any of these questions unless they have read and studied one of the set books thoroughly.

## 1 Make notes on the plot

During the course of your reading, write a brief summary of each chapter or section (if you are reading a book) or each scene (if you are reading a play). You will need to memorise some of this summary to use in the exam. Remember to use present tenses to outline the plot of a book or play.

## 2 Make notes on the characters

During the course of your reading, underline important information about the characters. Make sure you know exactly who the characters are, why they behave as they do, what the relationship is between them and what they each contribute to the plot, theme and to the text overall. Never make claims about characters which you cannot support with examples from the text.

## 3 Make notes on the theme(s)

During the course of your reading, remember that the exam question is unlikely to involve just retelling the plot. Often, you are asked to explore the theme; in other words to say what the book or play is really about, or to reflect on the meaning of individual episodes or scenes.

## 4 Memorise useful quotations

During the course of your reading, make a note of short quotations to use in the exam. Choose your quotations very carefully and make sure that the examiner knows why you are using them and what they prove. Do not quote long sections; do not misquote; and make sure you punctuate correctly!

Here are some sample questions of the type you could expect in the examination.

**a** Write an essay for your course tutor comparing two of the characters in the book/play and discuss how their personalities affect the course of events. Illustrate your answer with reference to the text.

Write your **essay**.

**b** A quality magazine has invited readers to send in articles entitled 'The Film of the Book/Play'. Write an article saying if you think the book/play you have read would make a good film or not and explaining what, if any, problems the film maker might face in adapting it for the cinema.

Write your **article**.

**c** In an attempt to encourage young people to read more, your local library is organising an exhibition on the theme of (revenge/unrequited love/betrayal) in literature. Write a letter to the head librarian recommending that the book/play you have read should be featured in the exhibition, and explain by referring to the text how the theme is developed.

Write your **letter**.

# LONGMAN EXAM SKILLS
## New Proficiency Writing

New Proficiency Writing covers every aspect of writing for students studying at an advanced level of English, especially those preparing for the Revised Cambridge Proficiency examination. Each lesson in New Proficiency Writing offers an insightful analysis of an exam task and guides students through the process of producing their own texts.

The New Proficiency Writing Teacher's Book includes:

▼ An overview of the Writing Paper in the Revised Proficiency exam.

▼ Useful 'Dos' and 'Don'ts' for the Writing Paper.

▼ An analysis of the task types that students can expect in the exam.

▼ A sample marked piece of writing with a correction code.

▼ Explanations of the marking criteria for the Writing Paper of the Revised Proficiency exam.

▼ Lesson-by-lesson notes with complete answer key, suggested answers and other helpful advice.

▼ Notes on how to tackle the set book option and sample questions.

**Components:**
New Proficiency Writing Students' Book
New Proficiency Writing Teacher's Book

Pearson
Education

ISBN 0-582-52998-0

9 780582 529984